MY FIRST ENCYCLOPEDIA

An eye-catching series of information books designed to encourage young children to find out more about the world around them. Each one is carefully prepared by a subject specialist with the help of experienced writers and educational advisers.

KINGFISHER
Kingfisher Publications Plc
New Penderel House, 283-288 High Holborn, London WC1V 7HZ

First published in paperback by Kingfisher Publications Plc 1994
2 4 6 8 10 9 7 5 3
2TR/1BP/0600/SF/(FR)/135MA

Originally published in hardback under the series title Young World
This edition © copyright Kingfisher Publications Plc 2000
Text & Illustrations © copyright Kingfisher Publications Plc 1992

ISBN 1 85697 263 1

Phototypeset by Waveney Typesetters, Norwich
Printed in China

MY FIRST ENCYCLOPEDIA

Our Planet Earth

Kingfisher

Author
Keith Lye

Educational consultant
Nigel Nelson

Series consultant
Brian Williams

Editor
Camilla Hallinan

Designer
Caroline Johnson

Illustrators
John Barber (pages 18-21, 28-31, 34-35,
44-45 & 58-71)
Jim Channell (pages 13, 50, 81, 86, 88, 90, 92,
94, 96 & 118-119)
Peter Goodfellow (pages 12-15, 22-25, 32-33, 38-43,
74-80, 100-114 & 118-119)
Kevin Maddison (silhouettes)
Larry Rostant (pages 48-49)
John Spires (pages 116-117)
Swanston Graphics (maps)
Ann Winterbotham (pages 51-58 & 61)
Paul Young (pages 26-27)

About this book

Our planet, Earth, is amazing. With millions of people and plants and animals, the Earth is the only place in the Universe where we know for sure that life exists. Our planet is very old, but it is always changing. Earthquakes shake the land and volcanoes hurl blazing hot rock into the air. Mountains are slowly pushed up and slowly worn down again. Some places are dry and hot. Others are covered in ice and snow.

Why is the Earth so varied? And why is it always changing? Turn the pages of this book and you will find the answers to many questions like these. You will find out how people use the Earth and how they change it. By learning about the Earth, you can find out how to look after it too.

CONTENTS

🌍 OUR EARTH

⛰️ LAND

💧 WATER

🌐 AROUND THE WORLD

🏭 PEOPLE & THE EARTH

Our Earth

🌍 What is Earth?

Our planet Earth is a huge
rocky ball. It is one of
the nine planets that
travel around
the Sun.

If you were in
Space, and you
could see the
Earth, it would
look like this.

The Earth looks blue
because most of it
is covered in water.
In fact, oceans, seas and
lakes cover about seven
tenths of our planet's surface.

The swirling patterns are white clouds. They are part of a thin layer of air around the Earth.

This layer of air is called the atmosphere.

As far as we know, the Earth is the only planet that has air we can breathe.

🌐 All kinds of places

The Earth is beautiful. All around, the scenery is varied. Some places are hot. Other places are cold and covered by ice and snow. In some parts, the land rises in high mountains and volcanoes.

Most people live in flat regions called plains. Grass covers some plains. Forest covers other areas.

People have changed the land. They have cut down forests and dug up grasslands to make farms. They have also built towns and cities and roads.

Amazing facts

🌍 The Earth is not a perfect sphere, like a ball. It is slightly flat at the top, around the North Pole, and at the bottom, around the South Pole. It also bulges slightly in the middle, near the Equator.

🌍 If you flew once around the Earth you would travel about 40,000 kilometres.

🌍 Our planet Earth seems big, but it is really only a tiny part of the Universe. The Universe is made up of millions and millions of stars.

🌍 The Earth is the only planet we know where living things can exist. But somewhere in the Universe there might be a planet where there is life.

🌍 The Earth is a rocky planet, like Mercury, Venus, Mars and Pluto. The other planets, Jupiter, Saturn, Uranus and Neptune, are huge balls of gas.

Land

▲▲ Under your feet

The outside of the Earth is a thin shell of hard rock with soil and water on top. This shell is called the crust.

Soil is made of tiny pieces of ground-up rock mixed with dead plants.

Plants get water and some food from the soil, through their root

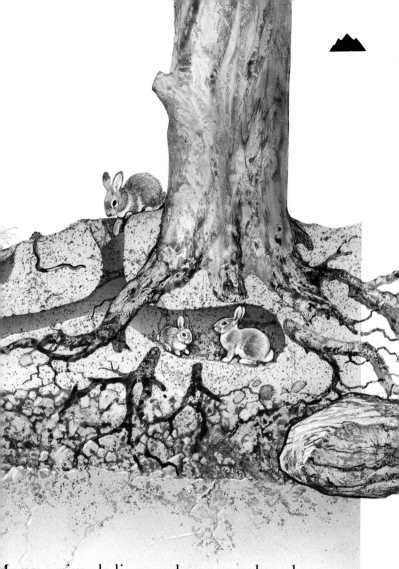

Many animals live underground and make their homes in the soil.

▲▲ Rocks

Wherever you are on Earth, on land or sea, there is rock under you. There are three main types of rock.

Sedimentary rock is made when layers of things such as sand and seashells pile up. Eventually the bottom layers get squashed together to make rock. Limestone, chalk and sandstone are sedimentary rocks.

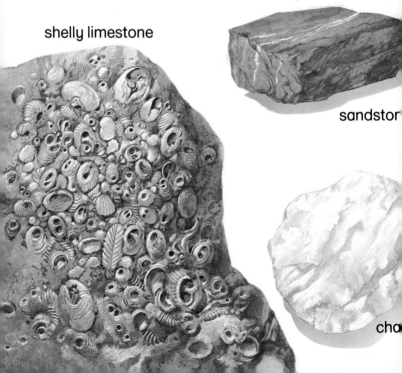

shelly limestone

sandstor

cha

granite

Granite is a type of igneous rock.

Igneous rock is made when hot, melted rock from inside the Earth rises, cools down and goes hard.

Rock can be changed by being heated or squashed again. This type of rock is called metamorphic rock.

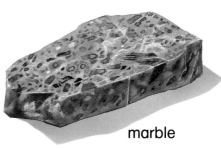

marble

slate

Marble and slate are metamorphic rocks.

21

▲▲ Record in rock

Many rocks form in layers, like a pile of sandwiches. You can see these layers in deep valleys or on cliff faces.

We can get an idea of the age of a layer of rock by studying the types of fossils in it.

1,700 million years old

550 million years old

250 million years old

Fossils are the remains of dead plants and animals. Millions of years ago, animals called ammonites lived in the sea. When they died, their shells were covered with mud and layers of rock. The shapes of their shells are found in rocks as fossils.

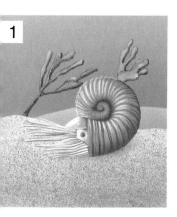

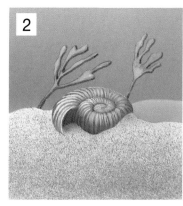

▲▲ Journey to the centre

The Earth is divided into three main parts: the crust, the mantle and the core.

1. The hard, rocky crust is about 40 kilometres thick under the land, but only about 6 kilometres thick under the sea.

2. The mantle is about 2,900 kilometres thick. It is hot, and in some parts the rock is melted. Melted or liquid rock is called molten rock.

3. The core is even hotter. It is about 6,900 kilometres thick. The outer core is made of liquid metal. The inner core is the hottest part. It is made of solid metal.

▲ Earthquakes

The Earth's hard outer shell is divided into huge pieces called plates. The plates move very slowly. They are moved by currents in the molten rock underneath.

When the edges of two plates move suddenly, the ground shakes. We call this an earthquake. Earthquakes can make the land tremble so much that buildings fall down.

▲▲ Volcanoes

A volcano is an opening in the Earth's crust where molten rock can flow out. Molten rock is called magma when it is under the ground, and lava when it is on the surface.

When lava cools it goes hard, and new rock is formed. Every time a volcano erupts, its lava makes another layer of rock. This is how some mountains are formed.

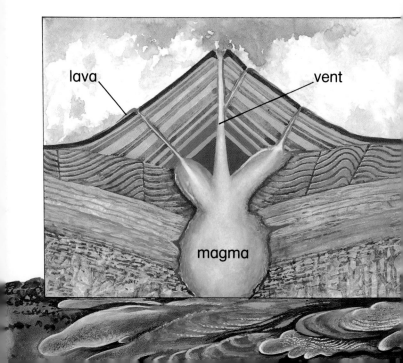

▲ Mountains

It takes millions of years for big mountain ranges to be formed.

Many mountains are formed when two plates push against each other. The rocks on the edges of the plates are squeezed together and pushed up into big folds.

ome mountains are still rising. They
ave jagged peaks. Older mountains
ave rounded peaks because they have
een worn down.

▲ Shaping the land

Things in nature are always wearing down the land. Winds blow sand up off the ground and rub away the rock like sandpaper. So the rock changes shape, very slowly, over many thousands of years.

▲▲ Inside a cave

Water wears down the land. Ocean waves crash against the cliffs. Rainwater wears out pits, tunnels and caves in limestone rock.

Sometimes rivers flow underground through the dark caves.

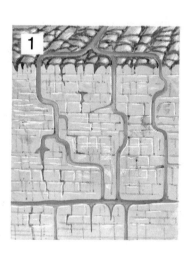

Minerals in the water dripping from the roof of this cave make stalagmites and stalactites. Stalagmites grow up from the floor and stalactites down from the roof. They grow just a millimetre or so each year.

Amazing facts

▲▲ The Earth was formed about 4,600 million years ago. At first, its surface was probably covered by hot, molten rock. This cooled and hardened into a crust.

▲▲ The oldest known fossils are about 3,500 million years old. From later fossils we know that dinosaurs lived on Earth 200 million years ago and then disappeared about 65 million years ago.

▲▲ The world's highest mountain is Mount Everest, in the Himalayas. It stands on the border between two countries, Nepal and China, in Asia. It is 8,848 metres high.

▲▲ When stone is worn away by wind and rain, we call it weathering. You can see weathering in towns and cities, on old buildings, statues and gravestones.

Water

◗ The sea

Most of the Earth is covered with water.
Many animals live in the seas and oceans.
Fishermen catch some of these for us to eat.

coast

oil rig   fishing boats

trench

The oceans contain many other things
which are useful to us. Engineers pump up
oil and gas from rock under the oceans.

Many volcanoes rise from the ocean floor. Some grow so high that they stick out of the water and form new islands. Some icebergs are as big as islands. They are pieces of ice that have broken away from a frozen coast.

island   iceberg

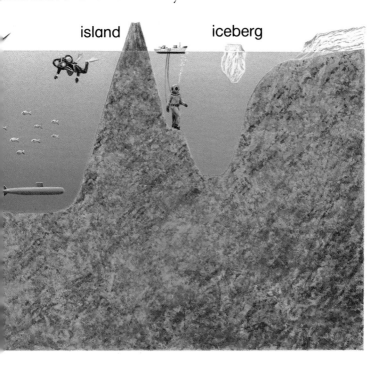

Under the oceans there are mountains, valleys and plains. The deepest parts of the oceans are called trenches.

◗ The water cycle

Water is carried from the sea
to the land and back again,
in the water cycle.

1. The Sun heats the oceans.
The heat turns some sea water
into an invisible gas in the air.
This gas is called water vapour.

2. As the air rises and cools, the water
vapour turns into tiny drops of water.

3. The drops of water form clouds. Winds blow the clouds over the land.

4. Water in the clouds falls to the ground as rain, snow or hail. The water runs over the land and soaks into the soil.

5. Rivers take some of the water to the sea. The water cycle starts again.

The life of a river

Rivers and streams carry water downhill to the sea. A river normally grows wider and flows more slowly as it gets nearer the sea.

Imagine the river as a person, getting older as it flows from the mountains to the sea.

. The young river

ome rivers start at the end of glaciers, where the ice melts. Some rivers flow out of akes or from springs of water in the ground.

A river starting in the mountains falls steeply and flows quickly. It tumbles down over waterfalls and wears away deep valleys.

2. The middle-aged river

When the river leaves the mountains, it flows in bends called meanders.

3. The old river

Near the sea, the river flows slowly across an almost flat plain. It flows into the sea at its mouth.

◗ Lakes and waterfalls

Lakes form in large hollows in the land.
Rivers flow in and out of most lakes.
Rivers bring mud and sand from other
places, so some lakes clog up and disappear

Most waterfalls are found high up in the
mountains. They often form where rivers
flow over steep cliffs made of hard rock
which is not worn away easily.

Amazing facts

💧 There are four oceans: the Pacific, the Atlantic, the Indian and the Arctic. The biggest is the Pacific Ocean. It is bigger than all the world's land areas put together

💧 The deepest point in all the oceans is in the Marianas Trench in the Pacific Ocean. It is about 11 kilometres deep.

💧 The world's longest river is the Nile, in Africa. It is 6,670 kilometres long.

💧 Where magma heats underground water, hot water comes out of the ground. A special sort of hot spring called a geyser can shoot out jets of water which are 30 metres high or more.

💧 Angel Falls in Venezuela, in South America, is 979 metres high. It is the world's tallest waterfall.

Air

☁ What is air?

We cannot see it, taste it or smell it, but air is all around us. Air is a mixture of invisible gases, mainly nitrogen and oxygen. People animals and plants need these gases to live. So if there was no air, there would be no life on Earth.

The air around the Earth is called the atmosphere. It covers the whole planet like a blanket. It traps the heat from the Sun to keep the Earth warm. But it also protects us from the Sun's harmful rays. Air is what brings different weather – hot and cold, we and dry, windy and calm.

Higher up in the atmosphere, the air has less oxygen and nitrogen, and it gets colder The air gradually gets thinner and thinner, until it ends and Space begins.

The wind

When air moves we call it wind.

Heat from the Sun warms the air and makes it rise.

Cold air moves in under the warm air, and a wind starts to blow.

Birds use warm air to glide through the sky. They hardly flap their wings, because the warm air carries them up.

Wind speeds are measured on the Beaufor scale.

Number 1 on the Beaufort scale is almost calm air. Number 4 is a breeze (about 24 kilometres per hour).

Number 7 is a moderate gale (about 56 kilometres per hour). Number 10 is a strong gale (about 96 kilometres per hour).

☁ Storms

Thunderstorms bring wind and rain.
But even fiercer storms called hurricanes
sometimes form over the oceans.
When they reach land, hurricanes cause
enormous damage.

Tornadoes are whirlwinds that form over
land. As they spin along, they rip up trees
and buildings.

☁ Lightning and thunder

Electricity builds up inside big, dark storm clouds. The lightning we see is a giant spark of this electricity.

Lightning often travels from a cloud right down to the ground. Lightning is dangerous, because of its huge electrical power.

Seconds later, we hear thunder crashing.
Thunder is caused by lightning. When
lightning heats up the air, waves of air push
outwards. This movement makes the
rumbling sound we hear.

We hear thunder after we see the lightning
because sound travels more slowly than
light through the air.

Clouds

Clouds are made of millions of tiny water droplets or ice crystals in the air. There are several kinds of clouds.

Clouds help people to forecast what sort of weather is on the way.

cumulus

cumulonimbus

cirrus

The highest clouds,
where the air is cold, are
made of ice crystals. They
are called cirrus clouds.

The largest clouds are
called cumulonimbus or
thunderclouds. They
bring heavy rain and hail.

stratus

Rain

Raindrops form when the tiny droplets of water in clouds join together. When the drops become big and heavy, they fall to the ground.

Plants need water to grow. So rain is very important for growing crops for food. Without enough rain, crops may die and there may not be enough food for people and animals.

Rice is a plant that needs lots of water. So farmers grow rice in paddyfields that have low walls to hold in the rainwater.

In very cold air, water droplets freeze around ice crystals and fall as hailstones.

Snow and ice

In cold places, water freezes into ice, and snow covers the land and the trees. A snowflake is made of many tiny ice crystals that have become stuck together.

If you look at snowflakes with a magnifying glass, you can see the patterns of the ice crystals.

Cold lands

The usual weather in a place is called its climate. Climate affects the land. Antarctica around the South Pole has a very cold climate, so it is covered in ice.

The Arctic around the North Pole is also covered in ice and snow.

But in summer some of the snow melts, in regions called tundra. Plants grow, and herds of caribou come to graze. Insects hatch out, and birds fly in to nest.

Forests and woods

Huge forests of evergreen trees (which
don't lose their leaves in winter) grow
in the northern parts of the world
where winters are long and cold

Other forests grow in countries with milder climates. Many trees in these forests are deciduous – they lose their leaves in winter.

The forests provide homes and food for many animals.

Grasslands

In places with long dry seasons it is mainly grass that grows. There are very few trees.

Australia's grassland is called the bush. Kangaroos feed on the grass there.

Many animals live on African savanna, which is grassland with some trees.

☁ Hot and dry

Deserts cover large parts of the world. They get very little rain, so they have few plants and animals, just a lot of sand and rock. Wind blows the sand into huge hills called dunes.

In some deserts, plant seeds lie in the ground for years. The seeds come to life only when there is a rainstorm.

Cactus plants in American deserts have thick, swollen stems that store water. So they can live for months without any rain.

The jerboa is an animal that lives in the desert. It digs burrows underground and omes out to feed at night when it is cool.

69

Rainforests

Rainforests grow in countries which are hot and have a lot of rain. More than half of the world's plants and animal species live in these forests.

The rainforests are in danger, because people are cutting them down and turning them into farmland.

Amazing facts

The world's driest place is the Atacama desert in Chile, in South America. One part has had no rain for 400 years.

Mount Wai-'ale-'ale in Hawaii has more rainy days than anywhere else. It rains there on about 350 days every year.

Hailstones as big as tennis balls have fallen from the sky. In 1986, some hailstones weighing just over one kilogramme were reported in Bangladesh, in Asia.

Antarctica is the coldest place on Earth. The world's lowest air temperature, minus 89.2 degrees Celsius, was recorded there in 1983.

The world's highest air temperature, 58 degrees Celsius, was recorded in the Sahara desert in Libya, Africa, in 1922.

The Earth

in Space

Earth, Sun and Moon

Earth is one of nine planets travelling around the Sun. It takes a year to go right around the Sun. The Sun is over one hundred times the size of the Earth.

Never look straight at the Sun. It is a hot ball of gases, and its light can damage your eyes.

The Moon travels
around the Earth
once every 27 days.
It is only a quarter of
the size of the Earth.

75

☄ Day and night

As well as travelling around the Sun, the Earth is spinning on its axis.

The axis is an imaginary line from the North Pole through the centre of the Earth to the South Pole.

The Earth takes a day (24 hours) to make one complete turn on its axis.

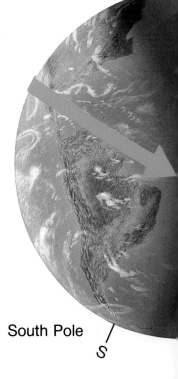

South Pole

S

The part of the Earth which faces the Sun gets sunlight. As the Earth spins around on its axis, that part turns away from the Sun and becomes dark. This is why we have day and night in every 24 hours.

North Pole

Paris, night-time

Paris, daytime

Long days, short days

The Earth's axis is tilted by about 23½ degrees. So, as the Earth travels around the Sun, first one half (or hemisphere) of the Earth leans towards the Sun, then the other.

This is why the weather changes during the year, in the different seasons: summer, autumn, winter and spring.

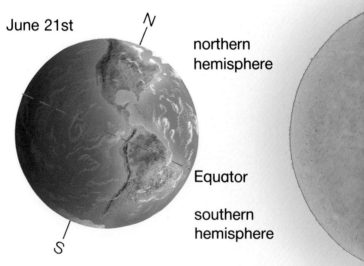

June 21st

N

northern hemisphere

Equator

southern hemisphere

S

The Equator is an imaginary line which divides the Earth into the two hemispheres.

June 21st is the first day of summer in the north because the northern hemisphere is leaning towards the Sun. But it is the first day of winter in the southern hemisphere.

December 21st is the beginning of summer in the south, when the southern hemisphere leans towards the Sun. But it is the first day of winter in the northern hemisphere.

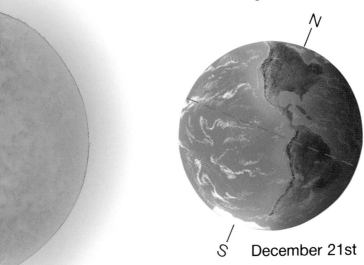

December 21st

So, the seasons in the south are the opposite of those in the north.

☙ The seasons

In spring, days are warm and nights cool.
Summer days are hot and nights are warm.

In autumn, the days become cooler.
In winter, days and nights are cold.

Not everywhere has four seasons. The North and South Poles have two seasons, light and dark. During summer, the Sun never sets. But in winter it does not rise.

In some places near the Equator, there are two seasons: a dry season and a wet one.

Amazing facts

☄ One year on the calendar is 365 days. But the Earth takes 365 days, 5 hours and 46 seconds to complete one journey around the Sun. To allow for this extra time, we add an extra day to the calendar every fourth year and call it a leap year.

☄ The Moon was formed about the sam time as the Earth. We know this because scientists have worked out that the oldest rocks brought back by astronauts are about 4,600 million years old.

☄ There is no life on the Moon, because it has no air or water.

☄ In North America, at Yuma in Arizona, the Sun shines for more than 4,00 hours each year. This is about 11 hours every day.

☄ At the South Pole, the Sun does not shine at all for 182 days each year.

Around

the world

🌐 Land and sea

Spread out on a flat map, the world looks like this. The compass points show which way is north, south, east and west.

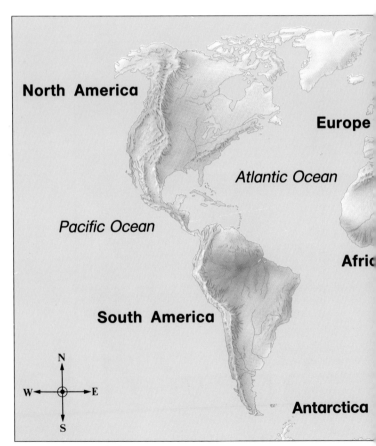

compass points

The Earth has seven continents: Asia, Africa, North America, South America, Antarctica, Europe and Australia.

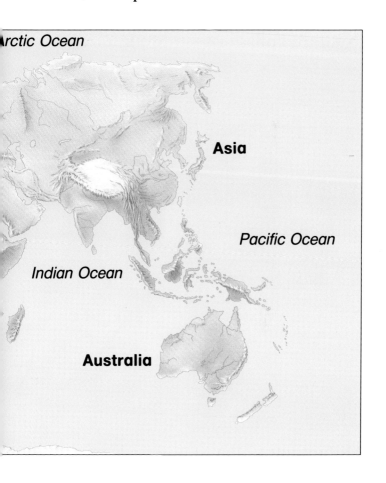

⚲ North America

Each continent is full of natural wonders. These are some of North America's interesting places:

Niagara Falls

The Rocky Mountains

Monument Valley, a rocky desert

An island in the Caribbean Sea

The numbers on the map show you where
he places are.

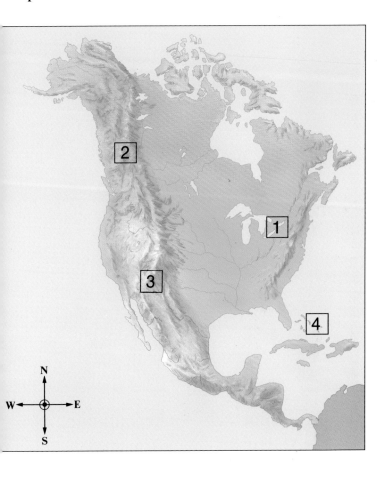

🌐 South America

The River Amazon, and the vast Amazon rainforest

The Andes, the world's longest chain of mountains

The Atacama Desert, the driest place in the world

Argentinian grasslands, called pampas

🌏 Europe

A Norwegian fjord, a valley carved out by glaciers

The Matterhorn in the Alps, a young mountain range

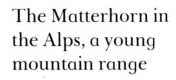

The River Rhine, which flows from the Alps to the sea

Coastline on the warm Mediterranean Sea

Mount Everest,
the world's highest
mountain

Oil wells in the
Arabian Desert

Rice fields in Japan,
a chain of volcanic
islands

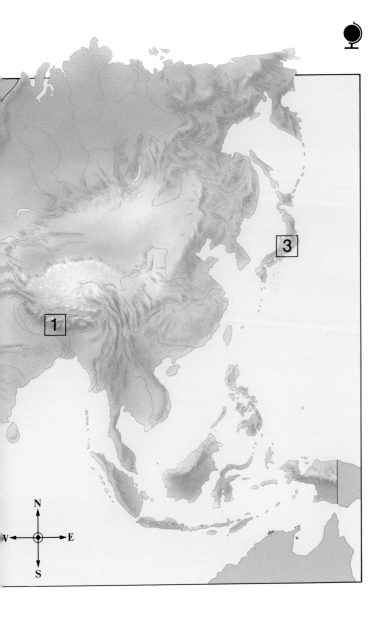

Africa

The Sahara, the world's largest desert

The Nile, the longest river in the world

Mount Kilimanjaro, soaring above the savanna

Victoria Falls, on the wide Zambezi River

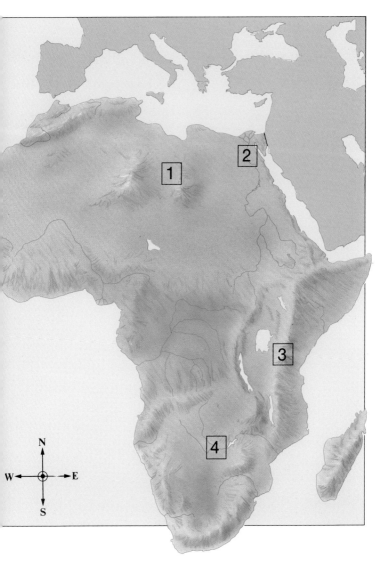

Oceania

A volcanic island in the Pacific Ocean

Ayers Rock, in the centre of Australia

The Murray River, the longest river in Australia

A geyser in New Zealand

Oceania is the name of a region which includes the continent of Australia, New Zealand and many Pacific Ocean islands.

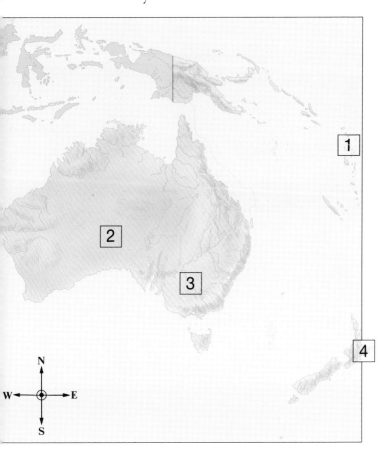

Amazing facts

🌐 Some scientists believe that all the continents were joined together until about 200 million years ago. If you look at the map of the world on pages 84–85, the shapes of the continents seem to match each other like the pieces of a giant jigsaw puzzle.

🌐 Australia is the only country which is also a continent. It is also the smallest continent.

🌐 The biggest continent is Asia. Asia is nearly six times as big as Australia.

🌐 The world has more than 5,000 million people.

🌐 China, in Asia, has more than 1,000 million people. No other country has as many people.

People and

the Earth

A changing landscape

People change the Earth. They often turn land which was once forest into farmland.

When people cut down forest, plants and animals which lived there die out.

Farming families often live in villages.
Other people come to the village to take
their children to school, do their shopping,
go to the post office or see the doctor.

Villages often grow into towns. People
build new houses on the farmland.

🏭 Living in a city

About 200 years ago, most people lived on farms or in farming villages. But in many countries now, most people live in towns and cities.

Cities have big hospitals, schools and shops. Cities also have factories and offices where people can work.

People travel around the busy streets by car, or bus, or train. Aeroplanes bring people from other cities far away.

⬛ Getting around

In some places animals pull loads.

But cars are the main form of transport for most people.

Trucks carry goods from place to place.

Ships carry the heavy loads
across the oceans.

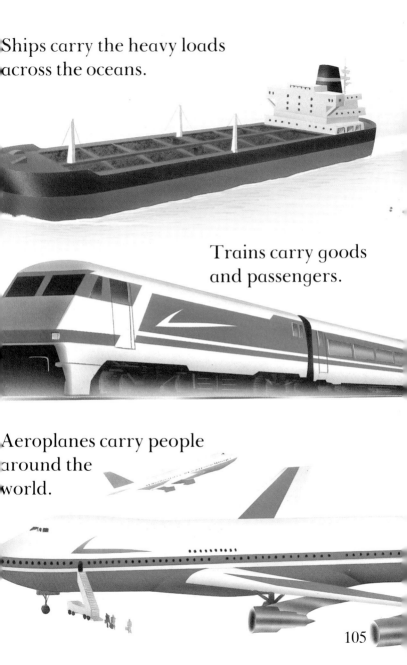

Trains carry goods
and passengers.

Aeroplanes carry people
around the
world.

🏭 Food from the land

The Earth provides us with many resources.
Resources are the things we need. Land is a
resource. All over the world, farmers use
the land to grow food for people.

The most important foods are grains,
including corn, rice and wheat.

banana

cocoa

apple

carrot

tea

sugar

coffee

harvesting
wheat

corn

rice

wheat

oats

⬛ Animals on the land

As well as growing food crops, farmers keep animals on the land.

Cows provide milk. Some of their milk is used to make butter and cheese.

Chickens lay eggs.

Many people eat the meat of farm animals.

Sheep's wool is used to make clothes.

Fish from the sea

Another important food is fish. Many kinds of fish swim in the seas around the world.

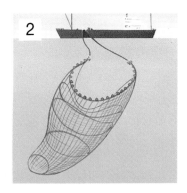

Fishermen use nets to catch fish. Their boats bring the fish back to land.

Timber from the forest

Forests provide timber for building houses and making furniture. Even the paper in this book is made from wood.

Rubber trees provide sap for making rubber. Tyres and gloves are some of the things made from rubber.

wood

rubber

When trees are cut down, new trees must be planted.

▨ The Earth's riches

The rocks in the Earth's crust contain many valuable things, such as the fuels we need.

Coal is used as fuel. Miners dig it out of the ground. Some coal mines are very deep.

Two other important fuels are oil and gas. They are found in the ground and under the sea bed.

Miners on a rig drill holes into the rock. Then the oil or the gas is pumped up.

![factory icon] Our rubbish

When factories and power stations burn fuel, they pump smoke and gases into the air. This pollutes the air. So do exhaust fumes from traffic.

Towns and factories pump sewage and poisonous chemicals into rivers and seas. This pollutes the water and harms the plants and animals living in it.

Farmers spray their crops with chemicals which harm the soil. And people litter the countryside with rubbish.

🏭 Looking after the Earth

Everyone can help to make the Earth a clean and healthy place for all living things.

We can help to keep the Earth beautiful by planting trees.

Trees provide food and homes for many animals. They also help to keep the air clean.

We can help to keep the Earth clean by being careful about our rubbish.

A lot of our rubbish can be recycled.
Recycling means making new things from
old materials.

These pieces of
rubbish can be
recycled.

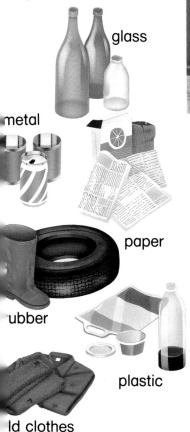

glass

metal

paper

rubber

plastic

old clothes

If we take our
empty glass bottles
to bottle banks, the
bottles can be
melted down to
make new glass.

Using things again
is less wasteful.
So recycling helps
to save the Earth's
resources.

117

🏭 Our planet

Since the start of the Space Age,
we have been able to see
what our planet looks like.

Space craft take
photographs which
show us the Earth's
continents and its
white clouds and
blue oceans.

The Earth is our home.
If we harm the Earth
and waste its resources,
we have nowhere else to go.

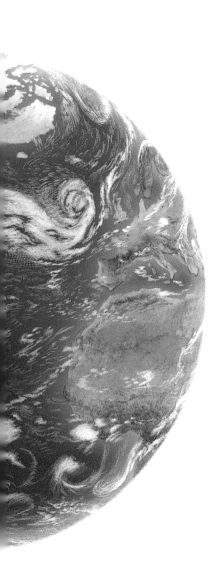

No other planet
has air and water
and all the other
things we need.

So we must all
look after our
beautiful home,
the Earth.

Amazing facts

Around the world, people are cutting down an area of rainforest roughly equal to the size of Greece every year.

Some scientists think that 50 kinds of plants and animals become extinct every day because their homes in the rainforests are being destroyed. Extinct plants and animals are gone forever.

In 1990, Mexico City was the world's largest city. Over 18 million people live there. That means it has more people than the continent of Australia.

Recycling one tonne of waste paper can save 15 trees from being cut down to make new paper.

INDEX 🌍 🌎

121

125